Jessie Cave

Jessie Cave is a writer and performer. She is best known for playing Lavender Brown in the *Harry Potter* films. She was a regular in Sky's flagship sitcom *Trollied* and has also appeared in *Call the Midwife*, *Black Mirror*, *Loaded* and *Father Brown*.

Jessie's doodles about love and her depiction of motherhood have a cult following. Her doodles and comedy were featured in Dictionary Corner on *8 Out of 10 Cats Does Countdown*. Her first book of doodles, *Love Sick*, was published by Penguin Random House in 2015.

Jessie's solo comedy shows have been critically acclaimed and have had sell-out runs in Edinburgh and at Soho Theatre. Her last live show *I Loved Her* can be viewed online here: sohotheatreondemand.com/show/jessie-cave

She lives on Instagram and Twitter @jessiecave.

A Nick Hern Book

Sunrise first published in Great Britain in 2018
as a paperback original by Nick Hern Books Limited,
The Glasshouse, 49a Goldhawk Road, London W12 8QP

Sunrise copyright © 2018 Jessie Cave

Illustrations, Cover Illustration, Photographs, Introduction copyright
© 2018 Jessie Cave

Jessie Cave has asserted her moral right to be identified as the
author of this work

Author photo: Bebe Cave

Designed and typeset by Nick Hern Books, London
Printed in Great Britain by
Mimeo Ltd, Huntingdon, Cambridgeshire PE29 6XX

A CIP catalogue record for this book is available from the
British Library

ISBN   978 1 84842 814 0

Woodland
CARBON
www.woodlandcarbon.co.uk
NICK HERN BOOKS
Printed on Carbon Captured paper

SUNRISE

a play by
Jessie Cave

NICK HERN BOOKS
London
www.nickhernbooks.co.uk

Introduction

I wrote the first draft of *Sunrise* in early 2018, in a hotel room in Liverpool.

I had gone away for four days.

My mum was looking after the babies – she had encouraged me to go away and have a chance to think and work.

I thought I would sit down and write some hardcore straight stand-up comedy. I told Alfie that's what I was going to write. I said I would be competing with him now, on the stand-up circuit. I said that and then sat down and watched half an hour of strangers' Instagram stories and searched for any evidence of Alfie with other women and then cried for a bit and then realised... I needed to write about him. And it's not all that funny, but it is all true.

I sent him only one bit for his approval. It was a bit in which he doesn't come across that well. He approved. He was creatively generous. He is my biggest supporter and my fairest critic. I think I broke his heart and he definitely broke mine but – he is my best friend. This show in many ways was written, well, just for him. But it's turned out to be something for me.

I also needed to write about the man who helped me (begin) to heal again after the break-up. It was like he was sent to me. He made me realise I can be fun. I can be new. I can have secrets too.

SUNRISE

But aside from all the crying in the woods, sexual accidents, Harry Potter conventions and Instagram espionage, this is a show about motherhood and trying to get stuff done.

My mum has five children and she does everything for us and makes everything happen for us.

I wish I was as selfless, giving and as patient.

When me and Alfie broke up, my mum saved me. She helped me with the babies' bathtime and bedtime most nights. She said everything would be okay.

When I came back from Liverpool I said I would like to have a sunrise backdrop for the shows and she started sewing immediately. I then said 'I think I need to have their faces sewn on to pillows – Alfie's face and...' and my mum didn't say 'Okay, you need to stop being so odd.' She started embroidering their faces into pillows, in the full belief (or mother's hope) that it wouldn't be odd and people would get it.

I've found the backdrop hugely comforting to look at onstage.

What this little book *is* is now the fourteenth draft of *Sunrise*. And I'm so happy to (over)share it with you.

Sunrise was first produced by Soho Theatre in association with Curtis Brown, and performed at Soho Theatre, London, on 24 July 2018, with the following creative team:

Writer and Performer	Jessie Cave
Director and Dramaturg	Adam Brace
Designer	Debbie Cave
Composer and Sound Designer	Adam Welsh
Lighting Designer	Sean Hawkins
Puppetry Consultant	Mark Down
Stage Manager	Ella Dixon
Producers	Steve Lock
	Sarah Dodd

It was subsequently performed at The Stand Comedy Club, Edinburgh, as part of the Edinburgh Festival Fringe, from 3 August; a full-length run at Soho Theatre, London, from 12 November; and then on tour around the UK

TO ALFIE

with thanks to

my mum & Bebe ♡♡♡♡♡

Adam - who has transformed the way I think
about writing + performing ☺

Ryan, Sarah Dodd (who is sunshine) and

Donnie + Margot (please don't read this xxx).

Have you had sex with anyone
since we broke up?

Why are you asking this –

I won't mind. Honestly. In fact I
want you to have had sex with
other people – on both our behalfs. I
can't have sex at the moment because
I'm guarding our children every night
but you can!

I feel like this is a trap –

Oh my god, it's so not a trap. Honestly!
I won't mind! I really won't mind! I just
want you to be honest.

Okay...

So – have you had sex since
we broke up?

Yes.

Right. How many?

One

Who?

Sarah.
She was in the audience one night –

Okay.

Okay, it wasn't a girl called Sarah
and she wasn't in the audience,
I just wanted to see how you react –

✳ When I was performing I would cover my face with the pillow of Alfie or Him
when they are 'talking'. I would hold them above my head or hug them to my
chest when I am speaking 'to' them.

1

SUNRISE

See!! I'm fine. I'M REACTING FINE!

Five.

Five what?

Five people. I've had sex with
five people since we broke up.

RIGHT. Okay. Who –

Just. Random women.

Five one-night stands?

Yep. I didn't like it,
it didn't make me feel good.

Okay, you need to leave now –

But you said you would be fine –

I am fine – but it's bedtime – I
need to get them to sleep, you
need to go.

Okay –
are you sure you're okay?

Yep absolutely – bye.

I didn't hug him goodbye because I was breastfeeding.

Then!

As I came onto the stage I selected
someone in the brave front row and quietly
asked them if they would shout out 'YOU
GO GIRL!' every time I pointed at them...
Sometimes the person I chose looked
annoyed, sometimes delighted. What they
didn't know is how well they shouted out
these three words had the power to affect
my entire performance.

2

I DIDN'T TEXT HIM FOR THREE WHOLE DAYS.

I wanted him to know I was hurt.

This was the longest I'd ever gone (since I told him I was pregnant) without texting.

I wanted to reclaim some power.

Every minute of not texting I was improving my 'not texting' stamina.

I blocked him... unblocked him two minutes later in case any loving messages he had sent don't ever come through because I blocked him...

I went running in the park, punching an invisible him.

I wrote in my Bullet Journal:*

(...*even though I only did it to teach him a lesson.*)

It turns out I would be the one who would learn a lesson!

I now know what 'REGRET' means.

Sometimes I feel like I'm waiting for my fisherman to come back from sea. The sea of pussy.

The fourth day of no texting came. I was in the park with the babies and my mum and I had this SUDDEN AND URGENT ITCHING NEED for information and thought 'I'll just call him up and ask him a few vital questions, in a fun way.'

---

* My mum read about the new Bullet Journal phenomenoncraze online and tried to get me and my sister involved. If you don't know what a Bullet Journal is, see my doodle and don't watch the YouTube tutorials because you will not be able to stop watching the YouTube tutorials. Also don't do what I do and get too emotionally involved with your Bullet Journal. They can't hug you back.

SUNRISE

I went into the woods bit next to the park.

I called him up and within approximately twenty seconds, I WAS WAILING IN THE WOODS... as a group of children came up behind me chanting '*We're going on a bear hunt*' as I howl 'TELL ME THEIR NAMES – '

we're going on a bear hunt

I'd cry and he'd say sorry and then I'd cry some more and he'd say 'I haven't done anything wrong but I'm sorry' and I'd say 'SORRY ISN'T HELPING. NAMES WILL HELP. GIVE. ME. A. NAME!'

But he didn't give me any names, and now I'm truly grateful for that.

We have a joint iCal so we can work out childcare. He basically just puts in his gigs. And when he puts in 'OFF' I know that Liverpool are playing and so I need to leave him alone to concentrate. To infiltrate his day sometimes I add in loads of pretend events so that his phone is bombarded. Like 'Release adopted tiger', 'Worry about inevitable things', 'Séance with ancestors', 'Orgy at Pret'.

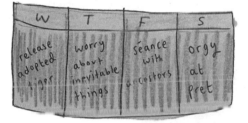

An iCal notification from him pops up. 'Jack's wedding.'✱ I was immediately enraged.

The idea that he will have a whole day OFF to go and watch this commitment ceremony – HE ISN'T COOL WITH COMMITTING BUT HE LIKES TO GO AND WATCH OTHER PEOPLE DO IT?

✱ This wedding was not going to be for another eight months. He put something in the iCal for EIGHT MONTHS from now when I don't know what he will be doing tomorrow. Also, I know Jack is a cool guy. So it will be a cool wedding and a load of cool women will be at the wedding looking for their soulmate. Alfie looks like a soulmate. I think he looks like one anyway.

SUNRISE

I was so angry I deleted the notification and then I thought – actually – I don't want ANY NOTIFICATIONS FROM HIM EVER AGAIN – I don't need him or his iCal notifications in my life any more! – he doesn't deserve to know my iCal notifications like I'm getting a smear test next Wednesday or I'm being a mentor for International Day of the Girl in nine months' time or I have an audition for a non-speaking but pivotal role in *Pokémon the Movie* on Thursday – I WANT MY OWN ICAL!

And then I deleted the whole shared iCal.

I felt empowered again, went back to watching the crime and paedophilia and nun documentary with my mum, forgot about it, felt calm.

A couple of hours later I get a text from him and my heart beats out of my chest and I think this is it – he's going to say '*I'm sorry. I want just you and no one else. Forgive me. Let's be a proper family who go to the museum together.*' I open the text and it reads:

> Ummm... did you delete the iCal?

So –
what I didn't realise is that by deleting the shared iCal meant deleting all of Alfie's gigs
and I didn't realise this iCal was linked to his manager and all of the manager's other clients
and in order to recover the gigs
the manager would have to reset everyone's iCals which would take many many hours and many many days
In short – I FUCKED UP A LOT OF PEOPLE'S EVENINGS BECAUSE I WAS EMOTIONAL AND IMPULSIVE.

I said sorry over and over again to him, thinking I've ruined his career. He was actually very nice about it. He's always really good and kind in a crisis.

I spent two hours on the phone to Apple Support trying to fix it but couldn't. iCals won't take you back if you leave them.

First Date ♥

...sorry, in your profile picture you had a beard.

I shaved.

I thought that might be the case.

It's quite busy sorry I should have thought about us meeting here – Soho on a Friday night – I'M SO STUPID.

No that's fine it's fine –

I mean you could have taken the initiative I guess – if maybe you had been on time like half an hour ago it might have been less busy but that's not an attack on you because you were half an hour late – which is arguably quite a long time –

It's busy, sorry I was late – but I have no explanation, that's just something I do –

Why am I so nervous? I'm not desperate! I don't need a man – I just WANT A MAN, DESPERATELY –

So we have a mutual friend I think –

Yep – I saw that too. Helena.

I went to uni with Helena.

I don't like Helena any more. Sorry.

Why – did you guys fall out?

No we didn't fall out, she just became really... self-assured.

Getting out of a relationship and dating again feels like I've just burned my tongue and I'm really

9

hungry but my tongue is still quite raw and I'm scared to eat BUT I NEED TO EAT – so I try eating and it's nice but I've kind of killed all my tastebuds.

You're really good at texting! Have you always been good at texting? Sorry – I'm a bit manic. I just found out that my ex-boyfriend has had sex with – London – since we broke up.

It's not the sheer number of people he's had sex with that upsets me, it's the fact that he has the emotional capability to have casual sex, whereas I immediately bring my memory-foam pillow and hide my toothbrush and buy him Fairy Liquid tabs before we've even said goodbye for the first time.

How do you stuff a pillow into a small bag so it doesn't look like you have a pillow in your bag and you're ready for a sleepover?

What do you do for a living?

I kind of, like, um, do a variety of things, it's hard to define really – it's kind of like freelance –

When do I tell him I'm a MOTHER – I have two kids, that I sleep with both of them in a superking-size bed with a wooden pen around it so it looks like a giant cage, and that just before I came to meet him I put them to bed and they did everything in their power to stop me from leaving and it kind of disintegrated my heart a bit and I feel hollow and like I've abandoned them – NOPE, JUST TALK ABOUT THE USUAL TOPICS! TALK ABOUT THE USUAL TOPICS!

Our Cage ♥

I should tell you now I don't like any
films or any music so please don't ask
me any questions about films or music.

I could teach you about films.

So many men have tried to teach me about films.

Do you want another drink?

I can't really because I'm on antibiotics
at the moment for a cut I have on my
elbow – I basically scraped a load of
skin off as I was trying to get two sports
bras off at a time – big mistake as the
sweat had binded them to my body...

So – anyway –

I've gone through your Instagram back to 2014 and saw a birthday Instagram you did in October and so I've managed to do our full Compatibility Report and – even though a Taurus and an Aries are ultimately well matched, we might encounter bumps along the way because I'm very VOCAL in times of stress and you kind of curl yourself into a ball like a hedgehog and stop talking if confrontation arises but WE JUST HAVE TO HANG IN THERE and COM-MUN-ICATE – I have printouts from cafeastrology.com if you want one –

your personalised spirit + destiny compatibility Lover report for an ARIES male and a TAURUS female

I think I'm enjoying myself, I can't quite tell any more.

Are you looking to have casual sex by any chance? Because I don't want to waste your time... And I only know one real-life person called Emma who can do that – she's a trainee architect and she lives in Acton – all my other friends say they are cool with casual sex but all my friends are wrecks. Big lying wrecks.

Anyway so I have two kids! A three-year-old and a two-year-old. I have a baby monitor in my bag along with my special pillow and I have seven hours before they wake up so let's use this time efficiently... tell me a bit about yourself.

I'm twenty-four.

Excellent.

What do you do for a living?

I'm a YouTuber.

EXCELLENT.

Sunrise Woman ♥

SUNRISE

I read this article about these 'POWER' women who are getting up at 4 a.m. to do all their admin and exercise and free-spiritedness before the working day begins – women who just want to do it all. I want to do it all. Sorry. But I do.

I've always wanted to be a mother, I wanted to set up an orphanage and have twenty-three children by the time I was twenty-three. I wanted to beat Angelina Jolie.

But there was a moment when I was sat breastfeeding with one boob and massaging stretch-mark oil into the other boob having just googled 'early stages of heartbreak' whilst crying – where I thought: '*This is not as easy as I thought it would be.*'

I Need To:

CHANGE THE SHEETS
for the 8th time this week

CHANGE MY POSTCODE
so I can get them into a nursery

CHANGE MY ENTIRE PERSONALITY
so I don't get upset by TINY
    LITTLE
        THINGS

KEEP UP TO SPEED WITH
THE INSTAGRAM ILLUMINATI
so I don't fall behind the pack

GET BODY READY FOR BEING
SINGLE AGAIN

BE SEXY

I go to this exercise class that is basically a treadmill torture session – sprinting uphill in a dark room with insanely loud music while the teacher screams abuse at you. You aren't allowed to stop. Sometimes I cry on the treadmills. I like it.

I listen to Dua Lipa, only Dua Lipa, 'New Rules'.[*]

1. Don't pick up the phone
(...*even though he's not calling.*)

2. Don't let him in
(...*he's not trying to get in.*)

3. Don't be his friend (...*but who else will I go for coffee with?*)

My go-to response is to always think I'm being rejected, and that now I have to prove them wrong, win the match.

I need to get through this, got stuff done, not blame myself, not let this break-up defeat me or define me – win through like I did at the Under-14 County Championships for tennis and nobody thought I would even get through the first round – I wasn't even seeded – but something just clicked that summer and I won match after match – all the balls went over the net, just, I suddenly had a backhand.

I WAS GRUNTING LIKE A WINNER.

[*] The only reason I got Spotify Premium.

I also had a few lucky breaks – one girl who was seeded and on track to win got stung by a wasp during our match, so she had to pull out. One girl who was also seeded had clearly just discovered boys so her focus was off – and in I swooped. And I won and everyone was like '*WHO IS THAT GIRL?*' and then I never won another match.

I decided I was going to try and be a Sunrise Power Woman. So I started setting an alarm at 4.05 a.m. – I gave myself five extra minutes.

The first day it was amazing. Even though both babies were still waking up multiple times in the night – at 4 a.m. they were meant to be in a safe two-hour sleep window so I made myself a coffee and sat at my desk and I did three emails I'd been wanting to do for about three months and I even started two creative writing documents on Word, one called '*Sunrise*' and the other '*Things I Wish I Hadn't Said to Him. No. 1: I DON'T LIKE YOUR MUM.*' *Even though I love his mum, I don't know why I said that.*✗

✗ His mum is amazing.

Day two was a write-off after a bad night where Donnie had night terrors which is when you shouldn't try and wake them but let the nightmare play out – so I just had to sit there and watch him screaming 'YOU BIT MY APPLE' for forty-five minutes at 3 a.m.*

Day three I was starting to feel the effects of almost no sleep. But I forced myself to get up, sat at my desk, had a coffee, started well – did another three emails, added to the '*Things I Wish I Hadn't Said to Him. No. 2: Calling him Therapy Boy when he suggested I needed therapy.*' Then they woke up. Alfie stayed over and said he would stay with them in the bed. I managed to do a bit more work, felt good but then I went in to check on them about 6 a.m. and when I got in there Alfie was asleep and Donnie was sitting up stroking the newborn baby's face with a dirty pigeon feather. Obviously I started screaming and 'OVERREACTED'. * *

Day four I gave up being a Sunrise Power Woman.

---

* Other recurring night terrors involve 'YOU ATE MY CAKE', 'DINOSAUR NO DINOSAUR' and 'I DON'T LIKE HELICOPTERS'.

* * I DID NOT OVERREACT. IT WAS A FUCKING PIGEON FEATHER.

Seeing Someone ♥

So I want to tell you something.

Okay.

I'm seeing someone.

Okay.

I mean – I think I'm going to start
seeing someone.

Right. So you haven't seen him yet?

Well, I have seen him once, face to face,
he was twenty-eight minutes late, he
knows my friend Helena, ex-friend.

So you're going to see him again.
Is that what you're telling me?

Yes.

That's not 'seeing someone'.

Yes it is, don't patronise me. I've seen
him once and now I'm seeing him again
and I really like his dress sense – he
wears lots of layers – you know I love
the layered look – so I'm likely to see
him a third and fourth time. Maybe even
a fifth time. I wanted to tell you.

Okay. Thank you for telling me.

You look hurt.

I'm not hurt – I mean I didn't know we
were meant to tell each other when we
are seeing someone –

But you aren't seeing someone, you're
fucking EVERYONE. Once. One time. No
repetition.

19

SUNRISE

Okay, maybe let's stop talking about
this kind of thing –

Why? WAIT –
Have you seen anyone twice?

Well, yes –

Who?

I don't think that's helpful –

I don't care if it's helpful – I don't
understand – how many times have
you seen her?

Maybe six.

Six? BUT THE BREAK-UP RULES WERE
YOU DON'T WANT A GIRLFRIEND –

I don't want a girlfriend.

Well six times is a gateway
to a girlfriend –

No it's not, it's very casual –

Six times isn't casual – does she have
Spotify Premium?

What?

Do you know her postcode?

You're upset –

Yes I'm upset – Have you shared an Uber
together? An Uber isn't casual – you will
have to have a chat in the Uber – that's
intimacy – have you eaten in front of
each other? Have you been for brunch?

We usually just have sex –
at hers – I leave early.

Do you go to sleep straight after
or do you watch Netflix? NETFLIX
ISN'T CASUAL –

We don't watch anything –

Does she have a TV?

Yes but we haven't watched it –

So you don't eat anything while you are
with her?

Um maybe toast –

'MAYBE' TOAST? You don't remember
if you had toast??? Toast isn't casual.
What did you have on the toast –

Why does it matter –

What kind of peanut butter –

It doesn't matter.

YES IT DOES – was it Whole Earth
Smooth?

–Yes.

That's the same peanut butter as me.

It really upset me, the peanut-butter thing. I
only got that peanut butter because he liked
that peanut butter.

If he's with someone else I don't want her to
have any of the same condiments as me.

21

International day of the girl ♥

I said yes to being a mentor for International Day of the Girl nine months ago thinking nine months is enough time to get ready to be a mentor but when the iCal reminds me it's today, I'm not ready.

I didn't sleep. Last night Alfie stupidly gave me a name AND A SURNAME of the girl he's been seeing and I spent the night not sleeping and using extreme willpower not to look her up online.

you go girl !

You had to arrive at the Southbank Centre at 7.30 a.m. which is ridiculous. Alfie came over at 6.45 so I could get there. He arrived and got straight into the giant cage thinking he could go straight back to sleep JUST as the babies woke up. I liked that.

I arrived and there was this long queue of 'together'-looking women in pointy heels and bags with no strap so you have to hold them with a long arm and red lipstick and they all looked like they'd been up since sunrise doing admin and Pilates. They all looked like legitimate mentors.

I immediately felt inadequate. I was in a multicolour anorak and pigtails.

We had to sign in and get a pass and everyone was speaking to each other but I couldn't find anyone else in an anorak.

I've never had a panic attack before but I was pretty sure this was the beginnings of a panic attack.

I must have looked odd because the organisers came up to me to check I was okay and I said 'I think I am going to have a panic attack on the London Eye' – which is where we were going to be doing the mentoring sessions. They say that my pod was the 'celebrity pod' and the *Evening Standard* were going to be on our pod taking photos.

SUNRISE

I say 'Is there a toilet on the celebrity pod?' they say no and I say 'If I know there's not a toilet nearby I get very worried – I haven't been doing my pelvic-floor exercises since I deleted the pelvic-floor-exercise reminder app – "Squeezy".'

They smile and say don't worry it's only forty-five minutes. Forty-five minutes? I DRINK A LOT OF WATER! WHY IS NO ONE ELSE PANICKING ABOUT THE LACK OF TOILET ON THE CELEBRITY POD? We could all get cystitis!

I say no I really think I'm going to have a panic attack and they say honestly you don't have to do anything you don't want to do and I say 'WELL HE'S GOT THE BABIES, IT'S MY MORNING OFF – what else am I going to do – okay I'll do it', and then they smile and walk away, powerfully.

We all walk towards the London Eye, it feels like school again, no one is talking to me.* In my celebrity pod the other mentors are Miriam González Durántez (Nick Clegg's wife) who was wearing the pointiest shoes I've ever seen and a fine MP and a nice woman called Pearl Mackie who played Doctor Who's assistant. We all smile and don't chat to each other.

We get onto our pod and the schoolgirls get on and then the time starts and we have to speak to each girl for five minutes – MENTOR THEM FOR FIVE MINUTES. GOGOGO. After the five minutes we had to move on, like speed dating.

I think, okay, come on, I must have something, SOMETHING I can help them with – I was a girl once – I wish this kind of scheme had been available to me when

---

* One girl DID actually like talking to me at school, but she thought she was a mouse and only crawled and stayed mainly under desks so not the ideal best friend.

I was eleven and about to be mentored AND CHANGED FOREVER by Avril Lavigne... Very quickly though I sensed that these girls ALREADY HAD THEIR SHIT TOGETHER.

I said to the first girl 'What do you want to be when you grow up?' and she said 'SURGEON' and I said 'Well, I can't help you there. NEXT!' I said to the second girl 'What do you want to be when you grow up?' and she said 'HUMAN RIGHTS ACTIVIST' and I said 'Ahhh, that's great! But I don't know anything about anything, sorry.' She said 'What did you do at university?' and I said 'Well, I went to two universities and I dropped out of – two.' And then I think she's going to say something like 'Well, the coolest people dropped out' but she just looked absolutely disgusted and said 'When can I speak to Miriam?'

I said to the third girl 'What do you want to be?' and she said 'Illustrator' and I thought FINALLY!!!!! I said 'Look. I can't draw arms but I can help you here!' and then got out my sketchbook. She has a look inside and doesn't look that enthralled and I said 'So I do doodles about love and relationships – ' and she says 'I get it.'

Then she shows me hers and it's AMAZING – LIKE AWARD-WINNING GRAPHIC-NOVEL-ALREADY AMAZING – and not just good drawings like really funny witty dialogue.

I think this page I'm looking at must be a fluke so I try to take hold of her sketchbook and look through – and me grabbing her sketchbook is the moment the *Evening Standard* come over to take a photo and the photo they took looks like I'm actively trying to steal this girl's ideas.

When I finally get to the toilets at the Southbank Centre, I'm bursting, I don't bother to close the door. I'm mid-wee when some of the power women walk in and see me hovering above the toilet I didn't want to touch because of germs.

SUNRISE

I wanted to sprint home but I was contractually obliged to do an Instagram about the event to tell everyone how inspiring and empowering the event was – how lovely these girls were – even though I found them quite hard work –

So outside the toilets there was a mirror and as I take the selfie, the power women walk out the toilets and judge me for taking a selfie even though they're gonna have to take an empowerment selfie in a minute.

And later we'll see who got more likes!

When I got back I asked Alfie if he wanted to stay but he said he had to work. I really wanted to drop down on my knees and say PLEASE STAY. But this time I didn't.

I tried to tell him with my eyes instead. I don't think he understood because he still left.

After I got the babies to sleep I was lonely and wallowing, and innocently checking how well my International Day of the Girl empowerment selfie had done compared to the other bitches and it had done sickeningly well – despite being basic and insincere.

Then I WAS AMBUSHED when the profile of the girl Alfie's seeing POPPED UP as '*People You Might Like to Follow*' – I WOULDN'T HAVE SEARCHED FOR HER – but now –

I really went for it.

Googling the shit out of her, seeing that he'd liked some of her Instagrams, I worked out that he'd liked them around the time I thought he was going to ask me to get back together any day now – I felt like such a fool.

I wanted to know everything about her – what he found so interesting about her that he saw her more than just once.

'She was fun,' he said.
Dagger.
'She likes a drink.'
Dagger dagger dagger.

The FUN was confirmed by her Instagram – she did look fun. She had a quirky mouth. He likes quirky mouths. I had a quirky mouth once.

Immediately I felt inferior because all her photos were of her with friends having a laugh holding some sort of cocktail. I barely see my friends any more. I don't hold any cocktails.

Then I saw a BIRTHDAY Instagram she did and I was fucked. Of course I did their full Star-Sign Lover Compatibility Report and OF COURSE it was a much more compatible Lover Compatibility Report than ours.

It even said '*These two can expect to ride off into the sunset together.*'

And I thought, well... I'll be getting up at sunrise with the babies waving them off.

second date ♥

I'm being stood up –

When does official STOOD-UP TIME begin? Twenty minutes?

It's been nineteen minutes. I'm having a pretend phone call with my sister so I look like I'm actually having an important business call and didn't even realise he's incredibly late.

Do I actually like this person? Or am I only going on this second date to make Alfie jealous – playing him at his own casual-sex game –

Why did I suggest meeting outside *Aladdin The Musical.*[*] I've even sent him a text saying:

I'M BY THE GENIE LAMP!

It hasn't delivered yet. That can't be the last text I send to him – what if I die tonight and that's the last text I ever send –

Hey sorry I'm late.

Oh – sorry I'm just on the phone one second – right yes um I'll have the second one.

Second one?

Oh it was just a... decision.

Sorry I'm late again – if you knew the reason –

TELL ME THE REASON!!!
Sorry. Tell me the reason.

[*] Still not seen *Aladdin The Musical* by the way – if anyone wants to take me.

29

I wanted to buy a new jumper because
I didn't want to wear the same jumper
I wore on the first date –

Ahhh that's – thoughtful.
Okay I forgive you –

Do you want to get something to eat?

By something to eat do you mean
a meal or a snack?

I could eat –

Yeah but do you mean you could eat
a burger or eight olives.

I'm easy –

I'm not. Maybe olives?

Let's get food.

FUCK THIS IS TERRIFYING. Do I tell him I'm vegan
or is it already obvious from my appearance? Is he
going to get angry if he's hungry? Am I here
because he just doesn't want to eat alone? I MIGHT
AS WELL BE A BOOK.

What kind of thing do you like?

Food-wise?

Yes.

Nuts. I eat a lot of nuts. I'm vegan.

You're vegan!

YEP. VEGAN. SORRY.

How long have you been vegan?

We honestly don't have to talk about veganism for ages – I'm not that kind of vegan.

Can you just tell me why you went vegan?

He seems genuinely interested in me. Why?

Ethical reasons.

I went vegan because Alfie went vegan and I wanted to beat him at veganism.

I just love animals too much.

I barely like animals.

Shit I think I could like him.

Shall we just play it safe with a chain restaurant or are you the kind of cool person who hates chain restaurants?

I'm fine with chain restaurants –

Great – BYRON. Let's go to Byron.

This will be the first BYRON I've been in with another man.

Does he have any weird food things – like I went out with a guy once who wanted to throw up if he saw milk. I had to pour milk into my coffee with my back turned to him.

But I'm not here to eat, I'm here to do things that are a bit different to my everyday life – I'm missing CBeebies *Bedtime Story* for this so it HAS to be worth it. I don't have time to scan a menu.

SUNRISE

Okay I'm sorry but I don't want to have
a meal. I want to talk and find out a bit
more about you and ideally have sex.
Or maybe not full sex but – I need to be
home by 11 p.m.

Great, I'm cool with that.
My place or yours –

Yours. Obviously.
Unless you want to sleep in a cage.

ARACHNIDS

museum ♥

* Whenever me and Alfie and the babies are out together I love it because it looks like we're a normal happy family.

Like recently we went to the Natural History Museum because we were trying to do a co-parenting day trip every two weeks – and no one knew that I was trying extremely hard not to ask him where he was last night because he didn't respond to my text messages for up to forty-seven minutes which usually means he's with someone – also no one knew that I had my fifth date with the twenty-four-year-old that night and I'd told him I just want to go straight to his flat and immediately have sex so I get back home by the slightly earlier 10.30 p.m. – ME AND ALFIE LOOKED LIKE A HAPPY COUPLE!

Well, I looked very happy, stroking Alfie's arm so people would think we were so in love and still so tactile despite having two young children – Alfie looked a bit unnerved about why I kept stroking his arm –

We went to show Margot the spiders because recently she's become obsessed with a spider who's been living on our kitchen ceiling – she says 'good morning' and 'night night' to it every day, has little unintelligible chats with it, it's so sweet.

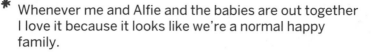

The spiders at the museum were a little bigger than our house spider though, and so Margot started screaming which set Donnie off screaming which made me want to scream 'WHO WERE YOU WITH LAST NIGHT?'

So it was less a pleasant family day trip and more a co-parenting lesson in managing trauma and not talking about who we're fucking.

* I'd been trying to do all my work in the evenings after they went to bed but that usually meant I got them to bed by eight (if I stick to my hardcore bedtime regime). I then had dinner while I watched Claire Danes crying in *Homeland*... I cried with her, then passed out, not before writing a list of things I hadn't done that day, including: 'Learn what an invoice is' and 'Have shower'.

What shall we watch?

I'm not sure – a series maybe or a documentary – let's watch a documentary.

I didn't think I was quite ready for the commitment of starting a boxset with him. Also I don't feel like I can watch any of my previous 'go-to' things that I used to watch with Alfie.

Alan Partridge, Peep Show.

The thought of Alfie watching *Peep Show* after sex with someone else makes me want to be sick. But he does love *Peep Show*.

I'm getting restless because I want to use this 'leisure time' when I'm not with the babies to learn things or have semi-aggressive sex.

What about *Stephen Fry in America*?

Perfect – educational but also, entertaining.

Now we're just sitting in silence watching *Stephen Fry in America* and this doesn't feel very productive – I should be at home with the babies.

Let's have sex and LISTEN to *Stephen Fry in America* – pretend it's a podcast.

We have sex to *Stephen Fry in America*.

As I was giving him a blowjob, Stephen was having a fascinating chat with a Native American Elder.

I don't sleep. He sleeps. I wish I was in bed with the babies but I can't leave now, he'll be upset. I always leave first thing in the morning so I can get back to them as soon as they wake up.

I go to the toilet.

Why do I always go out with guys with such shit bathrooms?

I miss the night-time wee walk I had when I was in a relationship. When you have to do a wee in the middle of the night and it's dark but you can do the walk to the toilet in your sleep – you know the route.

With this new guy I don't know the route yet and I wake up in the middle of the night thinking I'm in my old flat with Alfie and now... I've got so many bruises.

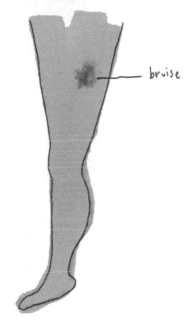

bruise

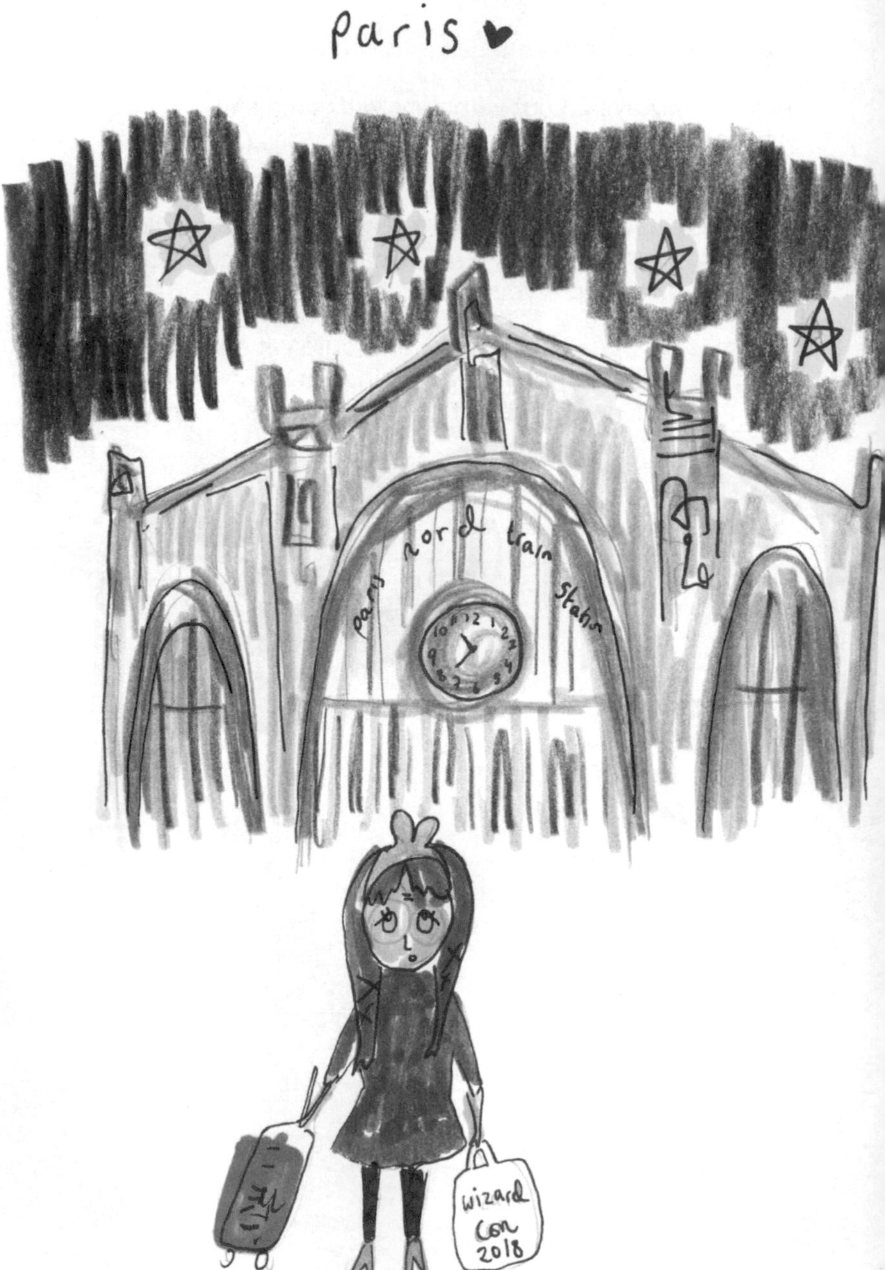
paris ♥
paris nord train station
wizard con 2018

A Harry Potter convention in Paris had offered me a plus-one for a four-day round trip. I really wanted to take Alfie but Alfie keeps reminding me that WE AREN'T TOGETHER ANY MORE! I'm so silly I keep forgetting. So I decided to take the new guy.

(OKAY! I'M WORRIED ABOUT SAYING THIS STORY BECAUSE I DON'T WANT TO NOT BE ABLE TO GO TO HARRY POTTER CONVENTIONS ANY MORE BECAUSE I LOVE GOING TO THEM SO ANYONE IN THE ROOM WHO IS THINKING ABOUT BOOKING ME FOR A CONVENTION PLEASE LEAVE NOW.)✱

We'd been seeing each other for about five accident-prone weeks. I really didn't want to go away for four days but I thought I should PUT MYSELF OUT THERE –

The trip was okay. The convention side of things is quite long hours. Signing photos of yourself you don't like over and over again and people asking 'What's your favourite spell?' *over and over again*. I always say 'Invisibility Cloak' and they say 'THAT'S NOT A SPELL' and so I say 'The truth potion then' and they say 'IT'S CALLED VERITASERUM' and then I say 'Okay – that one then...' and then they look very disappointed

People keep asking if the guy I'm with is my 'boyfriend', if he's the father of my children. I say 'No! It's just a thing... I don't know exactly what our "thing" is yet.'

We had a photo taken together. The convention organisers insisted and at the time I was like 'But me and Alfie don't have any photos of us together, this is not okay' but we did it, and I looked giddy in my Gryffindor coat and then I stashed the photo in my bag.

✱ OR STOP READING NOW! At one preview a convention booker from Germany did leave.

39

I have to hide how much I usually speak to Alfie – pretend I can't feel my phone vibrating in my pocket with messages from him about how they all have diarrhoea and a photo of them all on the sofa in the recovery position and I think OH I WANT TO BE THERE. Have to go on emotional autopilot to stop missing them so much – have a fun FREE time in PARIS!

He asks me what is the most romantic thing that's ever happened to me and I think about it for a long time and say 'Alfie let me sleep in on my birthday once. I didn't want to but he forced me to and didn't let me out the bedroom I banged on the door for so long I got tired and went back to sleep and in the end... it was nice.' I then realise I'm not a romantic person but he is and now we have to have a romantic weekend.

In the evenings he was keen to have a lot of baths together – I don't have time for baths at home. We listened to music in the bath, with the phone in the sink acting romantically as the speaker.

I don't have time for music any more either but I don't want to listen to his choice of Fleet Foxes for the hundredth time – ALRIGHT, FLEET FOXES, I GET IT – so we listen to my little sister Bebe's 'Love' playlist on Spotify.

I HAVE AS MUCH SEX AS POSSIBLE TO STOP ME FROM THINKING. Till I can't think straight. It's a holiday! I don't have to wake up multiple times in the night to feed a baby or have silent sex and then awkward chats with his flatmates about soup – I can

just have unadulterated uninterrupted sex with French news on in the background – the news sounds so much more sexy in French.

My sex button is on again – it's been off for the duration of me living alone with the babies in the one-bedroom flat and sleeping in the same bed with one in each armpit every night. My sex button also broke for a bit when I found my three-year-old playing with my vibrator under my desk saying it was a sword.

It was just me and him and a load of Harry Potter fans in a weird airport hotel. There were NO PEOPLE outside. Suddenly it was like we were the last people on earth... a hotel – the perfect place to have sex but I didn't want to ask the hotel reception if we could have a room for forty-five minutes before the afternoon autograph session begins.... It would be too obvious that I'm going to have sex for forty-five minutes.

So I thought – let's take a risk like they take risks in films and find a secret place to have sex in the hotel! We spent thirty-five minutes finding a place and eventually found a utilities cupboard.

I was like I AM IN PARIS, I MUST HAVE SEX IN A UTILITIES CUPBOARD.

We had uncomfortable sex for three to five minutes, tights and jeans down but not fully off in case of emergency – but that meant that when it came to putting one leg up on this step thing my tights had to stretch – so it was like using one of those physio elastic bands – my thighs were killing – we were just surrounded by stacks of toilet paper.

41

SUNRISE

It was lunchtime for the convention so no one was meant to be in the corridor –

But it was clear people were starting to queue up outside. This utilities cupboard was in the men's toilets. So in order to get out I had to exit the men's toilets. It wasn't ideal.

I waited for the noise of the queue to go down till I thought it was safe. I ran out and there were just two young girls in Hufflepuff cloaks in the corridor looking confused about why I was in there and so I had to pretend I'd accidentally gone in to the men's toilets, then go in to the women's toilets where I just look at myself in the mirror.

#harrypotterforeve

I was exhausted by the end of the weekend – I had overdone the sex, had too many baths, talked about too many spells –

 It was our last night though and so we really went for it. I had mistimed the – to cut a really long story short – he came in my eye.

Next morning. It suddenly felt so urgent to be home. I made us arrive at the Eurostar station early.

But he thinks we've got time for breakfast and enthusiastically finds a porridge bar on Foursquare.

In my head I don't think we have time to walk to a porridge bar but he seems really fucking excited about the porridge so I go ahead with it. We get there and choose from about two hundred types of porridge and it cost about ten pounds for a bowl and then we wait for the porridge and I get increasingly and SECRETLY stressed.

We only have seventeen minutes before our Eurostar leaves!

I try to say in a relaxed way 'WE HAVE TO GET THE PORRIDGE TO TAKE AWAY AND EAT THE PORRIDGE ON THE EUROSTAR – '

We get to the check-in and have to put our bags through – I get mine through quickly.

After handing me the porridge very carefully he then takes off his belt and puts his belt on top of his bag and then the belt doesn't come through the other side of the turnstile thing, it's fallen, he looks devastated.

My patience is gone now and my eye is really starting to hurt and now I'm beginning to think HE AIMED HIS DICK AT MY EYE so I shout:

'LEAVE YOUR BELT, I NEED TO GET HOME' – and we run.

We make it, just, and have porridge silently on the train. It is really good porridge.

He says 'Sorry about your eye.'

I say 'Sorry about your belt. And sorry I got stressed. I get stressed sometimes, I've hidden it from you so far.'

He says 'You haven't hidden it.'

At King's Cross, he asks if I want to get a coffee and I say 'No, I want to clock back in as a mother now' and we have an Uber back to our flats, stopping at his first.

At home Alfie answers the door. I try to hide my eye. He asks awkwardly how it went. I say fine.

Margot the baby runs up to me, ecstatic. I give her a massive hug. She immediately sees my eye and says 'Ouch' and she's just learnt how to say 'Kiss it better' and she tries to kiss my eye better – I say 'NOOOOO!!!' Then she pulls me to see the spider –

Sunrise

I AM SO HAPPY TO SEE THE SPIDER AGAIN!
I FORGET MY EYE HURTS!

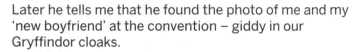

I go to the toilet to check my eye and when I come downstairs Alfie looks a bit red in the face and he leaves.

Later he tells me that he found the photo of me and my 'new boyfriend' at the convention – giddy in our Gryffindor cloaks.

He also tells me he's been invited to the Melbourne Comedy Festival for the first time. He'd be gone for five weeks. He asks if it's okay if he goes. I don't want him to go but I say yes.

Suddenly I think – is the girl he's been seeing going to Australia too? I want to ask him but I don't. I ask google instead. And yes, yes she is.

Immediately I start a list in my Bullet Journal: 'Ideas for Emotionally Manipulative Leaving Presents: Something to make him really miss us.' ✗

✗ At this point I asked the audience a direct question:

ANYONE HERE FUCKED ALFIE BROWN?
I won't mind – honestly.
I just want you to be honest.
No one? Statistically that's very unlikely.

It was quite awkward during one preview in London when a woman raised her hand. I told her to meet me outside after the show. She chose not to attend this meeting.

If you are reading this and HAVE indeed fucked Alfie Brown – WELL DONE!

Torture session ♥

SUNRISE

I think part of the reason it's taken me so long to move on from the break-up is I feel like I was unfairly dismissed. I want to go to a small claims court and stand up and say:

'I was pregnant for eighteen months of our two-year relationship – I was hormonal, I was controlling, I was tired – that TV you got was WAY TOO BIG – I just wanted you to do better, it doesn't mean I didn't love you – '

I've begged to get back together with him, so many times, I've demeaned myself,* done all the things they say to do in the 'HOW TO WIN HIM BACK' Google searches and then done *ALL THE THINGS TO PUSH HIM AWAY* in real life.

I had arranged for Alfie to have the babies for a couple of nights. I panic when I'm alone and not holding a baby. It means I should be doing something.

I go to my treadmill torture session.

We all get on to the treadmills ready to get screamed at but the teacher's not here yet – then a woman rushes in –

I freeze.

I know this woman's face.
She went out with my rapist.

I realise she's teaching the class.

Okay, so I should probably just say that I was raped when I had just turned fifteen by my tennis coach – he went to jail – I'm okay and I was okay quite quickly afterwards so I was lucky. BUT I haven't thought about it in a long time and I feel like seeing her today is a test –

---

* I try and perform this bit not completely pathetically to compensate for being a little bit pathetic here.

Sasha, I think, her name is Sasha! Then I check the board and it says Sasha. I'm right!

The class starts. I'm pushing my body so hard to try and impress her.

She seemed to only call out my name. 'GOOD JOB JESS' – I wanted to correct her and say 'UMMMM... IT'S JESSIE – I AM NOT A JESS!' but it was very loud in there. She had a headset microphone on –

She loved being the DJ while also teaching the class, she's obviously gone to a lot of clubs.

She said 'Pretend you're putting your elbow on the champagne table' so she must have a champagne table at home.

She held my feet during the stretching at the end and I tried to lock eyes with her.

Afterwards, people are leaving and I can't not say anything. I need to take this opportunity! She doesn't usually teach at this branch! TAKE INITIATIVE!

I went up to her and she says again:

Good job, Jess!

Sorry I know this might seem a bit odd but can I ask you a question?

Yeah sure.

She thinks I'm going to ask her about stretching.

I say:

I think we have a mutual – um – well, do know a man called ~~████ █████~~? – he was my tennis coach.

She looks a bit cautious and says:

> No, WHY?

I say:

Well. It's a bit awkward but he raped me when I was fifteen and I just wondered how he was doing now that he'll be out of jail –

She looks a bit scared and says:

> Oh my god, wow –

I say:

It's just I remember your face because you're really beautiful –

She says:

> Thank you.

I say:

And I think you went out with him or were seeing him???

She says:

> Oh no.

I say:

Oh okay. I'm just so sure you did –

She says:

> I can imagine how that must cloud everything in your life.

I say:

No – it didn't – I mean – I'm fine I just wondered what he was doing now –

She stares at me blankly and says:

Where was this?

I say:

Herne Hill.

She says:

Oh I grew up in Herne Hill.

I say:

He drove a yellow convertible and had
spiky hair like AJ from Backstreet Boys
did (at one point) –

She paused for a second then says:

I didn't play tennis.

She starts indicating the next class she has to
teach is about to start –

I say:

Okay don't worry.

She says.

Yeah, sorry.

I try for the last time and say:

Honestly I just thought we might have a
mutual – um – friend.

She says:

A friend who does that is not my friend.

I then leave.

SUNRISE

On the first morning of the trial we went to the Caffè Nero near the Old Bailey.✗

My mum let me have a blueberry muffin. Then she said 'Don't look that way, look over here, don't look over there, look over here – ' which meant I looked directly at where she was telling me not to and I saw him. She was shielding me from seeing most of him. But I knew they were his legs.

I was saying this story to a friend the other day and she said 'Oh that's definitely something you should bring up with your therapist.'

And I was like – umm – I don't have a therapist!

I probably should have a therapist. I probably should have lots of things. I probably should have a Nectar card.

The truth is I don't know how it's affected my life.

But that's not what this show is about. It's four minutes out of sixty, because I saw Sasha that day.●

I know having that happen does cloud some people's lives. And I feel guilty for saying this, but it didn't cloud mine... some people do get through it.

✗ I actually live near the Old Bailey where we had the trial. I've stubbornly never used St Paul's Tube (which is near the Old Bailey) because Alfie always insisted it was the quickest route into Soho and I said the 55 bus was. The other day I was running late and Alfie said – 'GO TO ST PAUL'S.' So reluctantly, I did. Take his advice, be nice, show I'm changing, being less controlling. I went to St Paul's and had the memory about the blueberry muffin. I didn't mind, it's a nice memory in a way of my mum trying to protect me – again. Now I use the station a lot. And it is quicker, annoyingly.

● Or four pages out of seventy.

SUNRISE

Ummmm – something is happening.

Yeah yeah it's great.

No – I mean something is happening.

OH YES, YEAH!

≪ we're having sex ≫

SOMETHING IS HAPPENING.

You're bleeding –

Oh wow!

You're bleeding a lot.

Oh brilliant!!!

I have polycystic ovaries so a period is always a welcome surprise.

Shall I stop?

Do you want to stop?

No.

Great! It's just a lot of blood!
I'm human.

Okay.

You can come inside me now!

Really?!

Yeah I'm not fertile because
I'M BLEEDING so it's fine!

SUNRISE

                                        Great –

Well I didn't mean straight away
but okay.

                                        Oh.

What?

                          Well – I think – well –
                        it's my penis that is bleeding.

WHAT?

                        I think I must have injured myself –

So I'm not on my period?

                              Well – you might be?

FUCK.

STD Clinic ♥

My period did not come. I thought I was pregnant. And for the first time in my life I ACTUALLY DID NOT WANT TO BE PREGNANT.

I was just getting to grips with having two babies, I can't have a child with a stranger – I mean, yes, my first child was with a stranger but that was different.✳

I wasn't sleeping because the babies don't sleep and then when I stayed at his I didn't sleep because he didn't sleep...

I was too tired to play with them and felt guilty just watching them watch *Peppa Pig* or *PAW Patrol* or *Dora the Explorer* or *PJ Masks*.

And then I was working and trying to do everything and be this cool new girlfriend... and also the cool understanding and supportive dignified ex-girlfriend...

And I developed a load of ulcers in my mouth and a few right at the back of my throat. Really BIG painful ulcers.

I went to the doctor and she took one look at my ulcers and said 'Have you been giving much oral sex lately?' and for some reason I said 'YES MA'AM.' And she didn't laugh and said I should visit an STD clinic.

Immediately I started wishing I had opened the weekly emails my mum has sent me over the years, subject titled 'BLOW JOBS WILL KILL YOU.'

> To: jessieisloyalandpunctual@aol.co.uk
> from: yourmotherisamazing@gmail.com
> Subject: BLOW JOBS WILL KILL YOU

✳ I got pregnant after a one-night stand with Alfie. We started dating throughout the pregnancy and on the day Donnie was born we said 'I love you.' I like to think we would have gone on a second date if I hadn't got pregnant.

SUNRISE

I couldn't face going to the clinic on my own and so I thought this was a good opportunity for me and Alfie to spend some quality time together, and make him take responsibility for his own very very CASUAL sexual activity.

In a way I thought it would be like a joint confession. Owning up to the mess we've made post-break-up. Own up to the new messes we are making with other people.

I made an appointment and we arranged to meet on the way. He overslept. He wouldn't answer his phone. I got the Uber to his flat, went and banged on his door and forced him to get up and get dressed – shouting 'YOU WILL GET TESTED TODAY!'

We get there. We were sitting next to this woman who chain-ate four Kinder Buenos and was having a loud phone chat about how 'pregnancy is funny' and I wanted to say to her 'Actually it's not that funny, it's very serious.'

We had to fill out these forms, he saw that I ticked boxes that he wasn't ticking and then I just burst into tears. I told him about my ulcers. I told him I might be pregnant.*

He looked sad. He always looks really handsome when he's sad. I wanted to tell him he looked handsome stood in front of the Gonorrhea poster. I wanted to ask him when he was next seeing Her.

* I can't be sure but I'm pretty sure someone was sitting in the corner of the waiting room wearing a Gryffindor T-shirt AND scarf... watching me... plotting some Lavender Brown fanfiction... hopefully.

It all turned out okay. Obviously even though he's fucked London he's STD-free, and I was all clean too, they just said I was very, very anaemic which causes ulcers.

I realised that since going out with this new guy I'd been missing a lot of meals trying to fit sex into my timetable. And for a vegan, missing meals is dangerous.

Alfie was so nice. The doctors were so nice, especially when giving the blowjob lecture. I felt much better and decided I needed to take better care of myself, which I've always felt is quite an indulgent thing to do. BUT NOT ANY MORE!

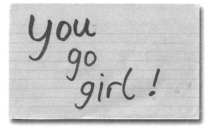

We were having this nice moment, I felt connected to him again, not in a romantic way but in a friend way for the first time.

And as we were walking out we passed a girl with headphones in and she smiled at him a bit too sheepishly and so I said to him 'Have you fucked her?' and he nodded and she just smiled and waved and she walked on by.

THEY'RE EVERYWHERE.

SUNRISE

When am I seeing you this week?

I um – I don't think – I think I have
to break up with you.

What? Why? You said you loved me –

Yes but that was – it's just you said
I love you and then we were having
such a nice time and I didn't want to
hurt your feelings –

Okay, so I won't give you the present –

I really wanted the present.

No – that's really sweet – you're really
sweet – more than sweet but I – um –
I can't get sick and not be there in the
mornings for the babies and I'm missing
too many meals – I'm anaemic now –

I can cook for you.

You need me too much. I already have
two little people that need me –

I can help –

But I want to do it myself. I'm sorry – you
gave me a holiday! It was like I was let
out of prison for the day for a walk round
the park but now I want to go back to
prison and I appreciate my prison.

Are you saying your children
are like a prison?

Yeah but like an optional prison when I
can decorate my own room and have
guests and have a job and feel fulfilled
and do art classes – okay bye.

Cardiff ♥

SUNRISE

So I've decided it's not fair to continue to have causal sex with someone who loves me because it's misleading so I vow not to have sex with him ever again. I go and get a full Brazilian wax because I wanted my vagina to have a new start.

Alfie is recording his show in Cardiff, it's a Saturday and I'm at the museum trying not to lose the kids. Again. Every time I go to this museum I lose one and start screaming the place down and so now the people that work there know us and stand by the doors as soon as we arrive so my kids can't escape.

Alfie sends me a text saying he's worried about his show and I think this is a cue – HE WANTS ME TO COME.

I joke '*I'm getting on a train now*' and he doesn't say 'WAIT – DO NOT BE ON A TRAIN' which again I take as another cue that he absolutely wants me to come and actually – he's insisting.✱

I want to show him I can be spontaneous and *JUST GET ON A TRAIN* and arrive and be like OH HEY I JUST THOUGHT I'D COME! And then have non-baby-related fun with him. SHOW HIM MY NEW FUN CAREFREE BREEZY SIDE HE NEVER GOT TO SEE WHEN I WAS GIVING BIRTH OR DOUBLE BREAST-PUMPING. And my mum could babysit so it was working out perfectly until I got to the train station and started thinking – what if he doesn't want me there and it's really awkward? – I thought NO – be bold, be confident! But it was the first ACTUAL spontaneous decision I've made in my life and I was now sitting on the train sweating.

✱ Here's where some people suddenly think – 'Okay – she's a psychopath.'

This spontaneous decision had already cost me eighty-six pounds for a return ticket. And then I booked a Travelodge room because I didn't want to presume I'd stay with Alfie – and I thought if I chicken out from going I can just arrive in Cardiff and do some doodles and have a lovely night's sleep in the fancy Travelodge hotel.

On the train I occupied my mind by writing over and over again in my Bullet Journal *'PUT YOURSELF OUT THERE, PUT YOURSELF OUT THERE.'*

When I got to Cardiff and checked in to the Travelodge and realised I was the only person on this floor NOT part of Jenna's Hen Party. As I walked down the corridor to my room, a few of the hen party were sitting there drinking and they looked at me and just laughed. One looked at me and just said 'Sweet.' I wanted to say 'I'M ACTUALLY HERE TO INITIATE SPONTANEOUS AND NOT SWEET SEX WITH MY EX-BOYFRIEND, THANK YOU VERY MUCH.'

I get into my room, lay out my pens, unplait my plaits, re-plait my plaits, which takes about five hours.* Put some rose Vaseline on and begin my long walk to the arts centre on the outskirts of Cardiff. Again, the long walk really giving me time to process my spontaneous decision.

The walk was quite long though so I got an Uber and then when the Uber driver was five minutes away I told him to stop because I didn't want Alfie to see me pull up in an Uber. I thought it was much more romantic to look like I've just wandered in and found him... at this arts centre on the outskirts of Cardiff.

I arrive and immediately see him in the bar with his manager, drinking. I duck and run outside, watch him

---

* My hair is long enough to cover my vagina as I write this. I would like to one day not feel so chained to my haircare regime. My kids sometimes use my plaits to pull me along. It's too long and it's not okay but then again maybe it is okay because I know it's not okay.

through the window and call my mum. My supremely patient mum – who has listened to me crying and complaining for a year and a half over him – who embroidered my puppets and backdrop for me – my mum says 'Just go in and say hi, he'll be happy to see you.'

But I'm scared. I watch him for a few more minutes and then his manager gets up to go somewhere so I text him saying:

He actually looks around and smiles. I text again:

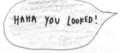

That doesn't deliver. Shit. His manager comes back. Alfie puts his phone back in his pocket. After ten minutes of looking odd, staring at him through the window, he happens to look up and see me. I duck again.

He comes outside. He's lovely. He's kind. It's all okay. I watch him do a good show. I'm so relieved and quite emotional about how it's a good show – worth the break-up.✱

Then we have a nice time drinking – I actually drink – and then I watch him and his manager lip-sync Beyoncé's 'Drunk in Love' and it's the best thing I've ever seen.

✱ This was the show that Alfie first did in Edinburgh (and then London) in 2016. We went up to Edinburgh Festival when Margot was just three weeks old and our relationship broke down throughout the month, largely because I was very very pushy with getting Alfie to WRITE THE SHOW DOWN and I made him get up in the mornings to DRILL the show and I became a bit of a, well, micro-manager. But the show was so good by the end of the month and it grew and grew and he wrote almost all of it down in the end. He needed pushing, but he also needed a girlfriend. Still, I'm glad I pushed him, even if it did lead us quicker to the... end.

His manager's forgiven me for the iCal incident.

It gets very late and it's clear I'm going back to his hotel. I don't tell him I also booked the Travelodge. He gets very drunk and I stop myself from wondering if this is a good idea.

We have sex! We don't have the babies in the other room about to wake up! I pretend I'm one of his many one-night stands. He always used to complain about me wearing sports bras so I've made an effort and I'm wearing my sister's lingerie.*

I notice he's got a few new sex things he never did with me before. An arm thing. WHO DID HE PICK UP THIS NEW ARM THING WITH? I should thank her –

He passes out quite quickly after and then I'm just lying in bed thinking YES I DID IT! I HAD THE CASUAL-SEX EXPERIENCE WITH ALFIE BROWN! I'VE PROVEN TO MYSELF I CAN BE SPONTANEOUS AND CASUAL AND I DO NOT FEEL HEARTBROKEN AND I HAVE CLOSURE! FINALLY!

Then I also begin to feel... pain. Like actual pain down there in my vagina. I go and crouch down naked and look in the mirror (in that flattering position) and see what I can only describe as many many red bumps. It's disgusting.

I immediately ruin my carefree sex afterglow thing by screaming 'ALFIE – THERE'S SOMETHING WRONG WITH MY VAGINA! HELP! I THINK I'M DYING' but luckily he's too drunk to wake up, so my carefree vibe is all he remembers.

I lie there in pain, not being able to sleep, I try to do the night-time wee walk in the dark and because I'm still a bit drunk I forget we're not at home and I walk into a wall.

* Thank you, Bebe xxx

SUNRISE

It gets to five o'clock in the morning and I have this wave of guilt and think— I SHOULD BE BACK WITH THE BABIES – so I get dressed and leave, like I was never there!

The man behind the desk at the hotel thinks I'm a prostitute leaving – so I say 'My boyfriend is asleep upstairs, I need to go' – it's easier than saying 'The father of my children who I just initiated spontaneous sex with is upstairs, I need to go back to my Travelodge now and then, quite possibly, A&E.'

I get an Uber back to my Travelodge, have a shower (make use of the room!), and then get the first train back to London. And as I sit on the incredibly slow replacement bus to Newport, desperate to get back to the babies, I google my vagina symptoms to pass the time and it's clear I have just had a bad reaction to the wax.

I sit there and think – NO... I DON'T REGRET THE WAX. And I don't regret coming to Cardiff. I am in *severe* physical pain, but I feel relief. AND I'M NEVER GETTING WAXED EVER AGAIN.✱

you
go
girl !

✱ Okay, I did get waxed again. Thrussian Roulette.

the pillow ❤

I was wondering if I could have my pillowcase back –

What about the pillow?

No it's okay, you can keep the pillow. I know you're young and you don't realise the importance of having more than one pillow yet – I just want the Spiderman pillowcase back.

Okay. You also left a bag of gum and a magazine –

Oh yes the *Frozen* magazine. I need that, thank you.

Can I see you again? Just for coffee?

I don't think that's a good idea. I want you to be free.

But I don't want to be free –

I know but I am doing this for your own good, think of it as a gift from a wise older woman.

You are six years older than me.

But in woman years, that's a lifetime.

He's perfect on so many levels.

He's good looking, he's sensitive, he's got a big dick, he texts back straight away.

All the things he's doing for me would be so right for someone else.

I would never hurt you.

66

I know.

We could be so great together.

I know.

You'll regret this.

I might.

I want him to really hate me now so he can move on quicker.

But I'm going to unfollow you on all forms of social media now so I can focus again – *

That's really cold –

Thank you! I've always wanted to be called cold. Look – you're amazing. You should be with someone who's amazing. I'm damaged.

But I like you damaged.

But I don't want someone who wants damaged.

What do I do now?

Unfollow me?

* I may have a track record now of breaking up with guys (three) and then immediately sending a text with something along the lines of 'PLEASE DON'T WATCH MY INSTAGRAM STORIES, MUTE ME, UNFOLLOW ME and/or DON'T BE OFFENDED IF I BLOCK YOU.' It's the kindest and quickest way to move forward in my opinion, I mean I guess you could be friends but – no, sorry! Ridiculous idea – FRIENDS WITH AN EX??? WHAT????? No. Sorry! Fuck no.

We get to the point where Alfie is about to go away to the Melbourne Comedy Festival.

For five weeks. In my head I think five weeks is enough time to fall in love with someone else, he'll come back married to an Australian surfer-model who wears anklets.

I always thought WHY BOTHER WITH AN ANKLET? Then I tried an anklet and I felt absolutely amazing. Sexy and amazing.

I've been working on my emotionally manipulative present ideas.

I dropped off some film for photos to be printed at Snappy Snaps (the best place in the world). I really liked imagining all the swathes of women coming back to his Australian flat one by one and seeing the cute photos of them on the wall and then thinking '*Okay this guy has obviously got kids and isn't looking for a relationship. I should leave right now before I cause any damage to someone I don't know*' (ME), but the truth is if I went back to a guy's flat and saw cute photos of him with his cute children I would think 'I WANT TO MAKE SOME MORE CUTE KIDS WITH HIM RIGHT NOW, HE ALREADY KNOWS WHAT TO DO!!!'

While I'm waiting for the photos to be printed I went to my treadmill torture session, and it was Sasha teaching again, still going on about the champagne table.

She's actually a pretty good teacher.

She doesn't call me Jess any more. She calls me Jessie.

There was this moment at the end where we all had to sprint for our lives and as the lights went down she looked at me and smiled, and I smiled back.

She even shouted '*YOU GO GIRL*' on the uphill sprint, which is a phrase I've always found quite – annoying – but now I find sort of comforting. I like her.

SUNRISE

I went back to Snappy Snaps and I decided on getting a little clock made with their photo on so he would always know what time it is in London.

I wanted it to be a photo of me looking amazing – maybe my headshot. I refrained. My headshot is too haunting.

I hid in the collage of drawings *they* had done for him (I had done for him) a note saying something along the lines of '*I will let you go now.*'

I wrote on the envelope: '*Open this in the sky.*'⭑

Then just as I was finishing the present – Donnie wanted to draw one more thing.

He drew a sun! An actual round yellow sun. He's never drawn a distinguishable thing before!

And suddenly my perfectly crafted emotionally manipulative present was RUINED – it was now too sweet and too genuine.

A GENUINE, NICE, GOODBYE PRESENT.

Now I feel ready to set him free... to fuck... Melbourne.

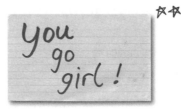

⭑ He told me when he got back from Melbourne that he only found the hidden note about two weeks in to his trip, so he did not open it in the sky.

⭑⭑ I would get the girl to shout for the last time, and then sometimes a few of the audience, if the show had gone well, would shout it out beautifully, as if they had rehearsed for weeks. And I would cry with happiness, because they got it.

jessiecave

I want to say THANK YOU to everyone who has come to see Sunrise and sent me nice messages afterwards - lots of people also going through break ups / single parents.

Hopefully I have written a hopeful story about a break up. And yeah... I have cried a few times ONSTAGE but it's been amazing to share my story. And everything is okay now... like my mum said.

www.nickhernbooks.co.uk

 facebook.com/nickhernbooks

twitter.com/nickhernbooks